Napa Valley
Impressions

Photographs by
Jerry Alexander

To all of you who have contributed the stories I am particularly grateful. Your stories are the heart of this book and each one was given to me with wonderful generosity. I'm indebted to you all!!

Napa Valley Impressions
Copyright © 1999 Jerry Alexander
Calistoga, California   USA

CHARDONNAY (OPPOSITE)

FOLLOWING PAGES

LUPINES, UPPER VALLEY (P. 6-7)   VINEYARDS, RUTHERFORD BENCH (P. 8-9)

JOSEPH PHELPS VINEYARDS (P. 10-11)   VINEYARDS, WINTER, ST. HELENA (P.12-13)

Printed in Thailand by Amarin Printing and Publishing
E-mail: info@amarin.co.th.   Phone No. (662) 8821010   Fax No. (662) 433-2742, (662) 434-1385

PHOTOGRAPH BY LOMA ALEXANDER

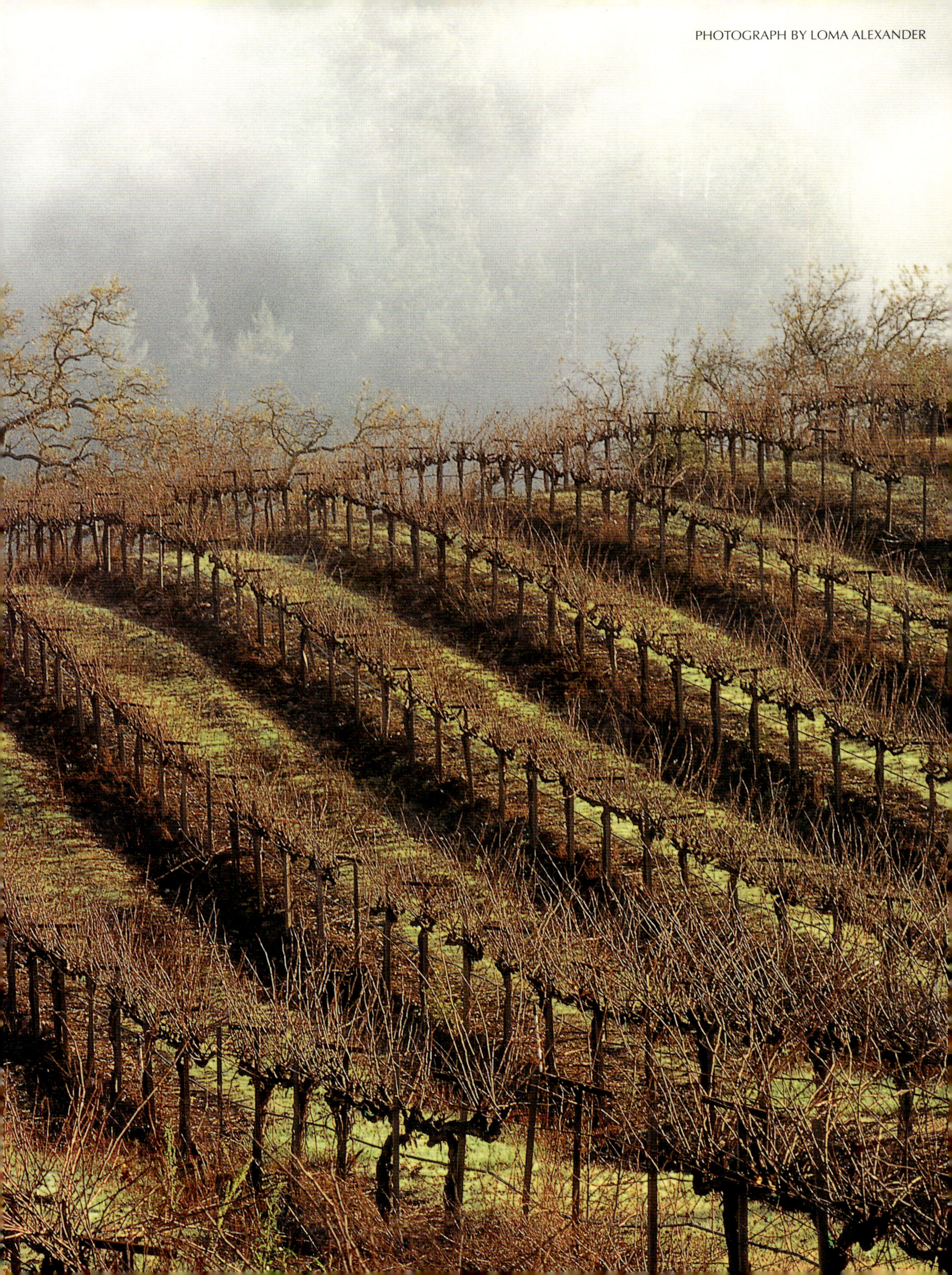

Duck on Pond

Robin Lail

The Chinese labor force made substantial contributions to the Napa Valley during the second half of the 1880's. They were the primary builders of the railroad, worked in the vineyards and the wineries, and many of the stone walls which they built remain today as monuments to their hours of heavy toil.

There were numerous Chinese employees at Inglenook during the tenure of Captain Gustav Niebaum. This certainly was a rigorous place of employment, and among other things, they planted the firs and eucalyptus as seedlings one by one on the hillsides surrounding Inglenook and are beautiful and lasting contributions to the Napa Valley. Their daily responsibilities included sweeping the one mile driveway from the house to the highway. Captain Niebaum was a meticulous man and conducted white glove inspections of the winery frequently. It was the job of the Chinese cellar works to be sure his gloves were still spotless at the end of the inspections.

The Niebaums also enjoyed the services of a Chinese cook, who was known as "Cook Sing." As Cook Sing grew older, his pace slowed noticeably, until it finally seemed to Mrs. Niebaum that he was hardly moving at all. She decided to speak with him about this turn of events, and summoned him to the dining room one morning after the breakfast had been cleared.

An imposing and formal Victorian woman, Susan Niebaum sat stiffly at the far end of the table and gazed at Sing. "Cook Sing," she said, "we are very concerned about you. Frankly, you don't seem to be doing much of anything, and your work is unsatisfactory. We know that you are getting older, but you must do your job or we shall have to think about making a change." Unfazed Cook Sing beamed at Mrs. Niebaum. "Ah, Mrs. Niebaum," he exclaimed, "Cook Sing like duck on pond. On the surface all is calm. But underneath feet going all the time!"

Not too surprisingly no change was made, and Cook Sing lived as a beloved member of the Niebaum household until the end of his days.

Transitions

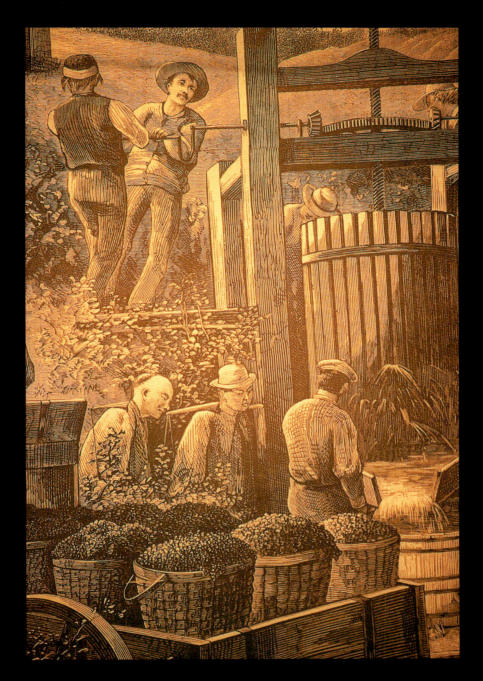

Transitions

Lin Weber, *Napa Valley Historian*

Just as wine goes through many stages in its life cycle throughout the year, so has the Napa Valley's population undergone a series of dramatic transitions. In its many-layered demographic history, some ethnic groups are still present and vital in the community, but others have vanished with scarcely a trace.

The very first people to make this place their home referred to it as Talahalusi, "Beautiful Valley" and called themselves Onasti, the "outspoken people." They may have arrived here as long ago as 10,000 years BC and were certainly here 6,000 years ago. An offshoot of today's Yukian people, they spoke what many linguists say is the oldest indigenous language in California. They were diminutive by today's standards, the men averaging under 5'5". The men wore clothing in the winter, for warmth, but otherwise nothing at all, and the women dressed in apron-like jumpers woven from grasses or cut from fur. Where these primitive people came from, no one is certain; the people themselves had no migration myth. In their own account of their origins, they said that Taikomol, the Creator, laid down sticks in the house of Coyote: big sticks for men and smaller ones for women. Taikomol produced children by scattering little sticks around the larger ones. Coyote taught them to fish and hunt and to gather the acorns upon which their economy was based. In time the Yuki-speakers were pressed in by competing native groups who migrated to the area from the East, North and South. They became warlike, defending their paradise from intruders.

They had no real defense, however, against the Mexican soldiers who arrived ready for battle in layers of leather armor in 1823. When the native people resisted the soldiers' efforts to convert them to Christianity, the soldiers called them Guapo, "courageous" (also "handsome"). The name was popularized to "Wappo," and the Valley's oldest residents had a new name. The Valley itself was also renamed. "Napa" is derived from Napato, a community of natives that once flourished somewhere in the Valley, one of the many little villages to be absorbed into San Francisco de Solano, the mission in what is now Sonoma.

Most of the soldiers and Mexican settlers lived around the garrison and used the Napa Valley to run their cattle and horses, both of which the threatened natives attempted to steal for food. Recrimination for such thefts was harsh. It was disease however, that wreaked the greatest havoc on the Wappo. An epidemic of smallpox decimated the native population in 1837, just as the first men and women of European descent began to settle here.

The entire Napa Valley became a domain of oaks and wild grasses, shared by a handful of families in good standing with the Mexican administrator, General Mariano Vallejo. Nine Mexicans, three Americans and an Englishman received

land grants between 1836 and 1846, but only a few of them actually lived here. A scattering of others—greasy fur trappers and sailors who jumped ship—also passed through. In 1841 however, a party of American adventurers found their way across the Sierra, and several of these intrepids (including a woman and a toddler) made permanent camps in the Up-Valley, near what is now Calistoga. They were followed by others, some of whom brought wagons full of household goods and an ambition to settle down forever. The trickle of emigrants soon became a steady stream.

1846 was a watershed year for the Napa Valley. Two important events took place, one of great local significance, the other an event with international ramifications. Winter came early and hard that year, and one of the emigrant groups trying to cross the Sierra into California became snowbound. Known to history as "the Donner Party," this unfortunate band of nearly 100 hopeful settlers was rescued in large part by volunteers who lived or would soon live in the Napa Valley. Many of the Donner Party's survivors came to the Valley to recuperate, and some put down roots and made their home here. One Donner Party member, Sarah Fosdick Graves, opened the second school in California.

The other more significant transition that took place that year was precipitated by the daring and at times burlesque Bear Flag Revolt, much of which was organized and manned by Napa Valley pioneers. Dressed in buckskins and wild-eyed with excitement, some 35 Americans stormed the Sonoma home of General Vallejo and took over the garrison without a shot. They used berry juice and makeshift paintbrushes to create a flag that featured a bear looking up at a star. A variation of their victory banner is now the state flag of California. Luckily for them, an American Army lieutenant, John C. Fremont, was nearby with a host of well-armed men, and the US Navy had warships in the Pacific. The Mexican-American War, which also started in 1846, caught fire in California, but only after the Bear Flaggers conquered Sonoma.

In one of the most stupendous instances of synchronicity in history, just nine days after the war between Mexico and the United States ended, gold was discovered in the Sierra foothills.

Many of the Valley's earliest pioneers were among the first to strike it rich in "the digs." Napa City (as it was called back then, now simplified to Napa) was a wintering place for gold miners. Odd-looking wood and canvas shanties sprung up all over town. Saloons were everywhere, but so were backers of prohibition, even in the 1850's. Lynchings and governmental corruption were the order of the day, and Napa City had its share of low doings in high places.

Farmers cleared the shoulder-high wild grasses that abounded in the Valley and prepared homesteads for their big families in Napa City and the Up-Valley area near what is now Bothe State Park. Two of the earliest pioneers, John York and David Hudson, discovered a lush canyon that was alive with hot, sulfurous springs. They sold their find to some entrepreneurial developers who created California's first resort, White Sulphur Springs. Shortly afterward, not far away, a town began. The residents there decided to call it "St. Helena," but the entire area was referred to on maps as "Hot Springs Township."

Many other resorts appeared in the Napa Valley, most notably "Calistoga Hot Springs," a mini-wonderland founded by a schemer named Sam Brannan. The town of Calistoga formed around Brannan's imaginative resort.

The resorts attracted a segment of the population that is still an important element in the area: tourists. There were two groups of people who could afford to summer in style in the spas of 19th Century Napa Valley: young San Francisco's newly rich and those with "old money," mostly pioneers from aristocratic southern families who had come West. Many of these visitors had sophisticated tastes and sensed in the Valley's Mediterranean climate the potential to provide something they had learned to value: good wine.

A political refugee from Prussia, Charles Krug, also sensed that potential. After learning the basics from another refugee, a Hungarian named Agostin Haraszthy, in 1858 Krug crushed the first grapes grown in the Napa Valley for commercial purposes, those of an English expatriate named John Patchett. George Beldon Crane, an American, also experimented with winemaking, as did a few other American pioneers. It was the Napa Valley's European emigrants, however, who had the greatest impact on what would become the area's most important industry. In the 1860's and 70's, another layer of what would be part of the Napa Valley's demographic bedrock, immigrants from Western Europe poured into the Valley. German, Swiss, Italian, and French families came by the hundreds to this idyllic land of opportunity in the Far West. And most of them planted grapes.

Winemaking, however, was not the only endeavor that captured the imagination of the Valley's first settlers. The region's turbulent volcanic past, which created a perfect terroir for viticulture, had also created treasures underground. The Valley's superficial resemblance to the Sierra foothills helped spark a series of gold and silver rushes in the 1850's and 60's. The result was one meaningful find of the shiny stuff, but the accidental discovery of another substance useful in mining, the creation of explosives and certain nautical and scientific needs: cinnabar, also called quicksilver, but more commonly known today as mercury. Napa County engaged extensively in cinnabar mining, and many of the Valley's more

OLD BALE GRIST MILL

CAVES AT SCHRAMSBERG

fortunate pioneers were able to consolidate their wealth by investing as partners in these enterprises.

Mining was difficult and dangerous. To do the work, the mine owners depended on another group of pioneers: the Chinese. Chinese men who had come to California to find gold and then to labor on the railroads found work in the Napa Valley as miners. As many as 900 Chinese men lived in a Chinatown just south of St. Helena. Three hundred more lived in a Chinatown at the foot of Second Street in Napa City, and other, smaller Chinatowns grew up in Calistoga, Rutherford, and Pope Valley. The Chinese were subjected to excruciating discrimination, not only informally and through the Napa Valley press, but legally, in the form of xenophobic legislation aimed at driving this part of the population out of the country. Like the Wappo, the Chinese all but vanished from the Napa Valley, as did the cinnabar industry.

Meanwhile, the wine industry, battling bad weather, vintners' inexperience, an unpredictable economy and a horrible bug named "phylloxera," hung on. As the 19th Century wore down, California wines slowly but surely gained international recognition. Winemaking eventually became associated with money-making, and scores of wineries, big and small, fermented the grape up and down the valley. Italians in Napa and Italian Swiss in the Up-Valley played an especially important part in the industry's success, although Northern Europeans and Americans also made names for themselves as vintners. Families who had earned fortunes in other businesses built elaborate mansions in the Napa Valley and operated wineries as hobbies. For a rural region, the Napa Valley of the early 20th Century was surprisingly upper crust.

The conscience of the nation, however, was unsettled in the first part of the new century. Times were hard. There had been a Great War; influenza had ravished the populace. Aroused by the writings of journalists who exposed the abuses of Big Business, and drawn to outrage over the treatment of women and to other social issues, many reformers began to search for a culprit to blame for life's difficulties. In 1919, American voters decided that the villain was alcohol. The

COURTESY OF SUTTER HOME WINERY

Volstead Act was passed, prohibiting the production, sale and transportation of alcoholic beverages for other than religious purposes.

Prohibition was to the wine business what smallpox had been to the Wappo and xenophobia to the Chinese. In a stroke, the entire industry was nearly obliterated. Some vintners bootlegged, and a few stalwarts eked out a living by making sacramental wines, but most plowed their carefully grafted, phylloxera-resistant vines, and hence their fortunes, under the ground. What had once been a sea of *vitis vinifera* became orchards of prune and walnut. Cattle once again roamed the grassy hills in great numbers. Vines overtook the wineries of the last century. Many rotted away, their names forgotten. When the devastating Act was finally repealed in December, 1933, the generation of pioneer winemakers had passed away, and the wonderful art was lost.

Like Sleeping Beauty, the Valley fell into a lovely but very quiet and prolonged agricultural slumber. The Napa Valley's elegant past remained as a dim half-memory for decades. Old stone mansions and old stone wineries seemed to whisper secrets of a former glory, and even though a few vintners returned to their families' enology traditions, the product was often disappointing. It wasn't until the early 1970's that the industry was kissed by modern advances in the art of winemaking—and woke up.

The Prince who brought the wine industry back to life may have been Corporate Enterprise. The Nestle Company of Switzerland, Moet Chandon of France, and the Heublein Corporation were among the larger names to take an interest in developing the Valley's most obvious resource. Local banks also played a helpful role in supporting the endeavors of the Valley's new pioneers. The other great awakener was a local resident, Robert Mondavi. Mondavi saw the Valley's unique potential to produce a premium product that would be recognized world wide. Serving as informal ambassador to the great wine growing regions of the world, Mondavi, like Charles Krug a hundred years earlier, was a prime mover in the industry's resurrection.

Enology and viticulture once again became important subjects of study. Winemakers and growers eagerly shared the results of their labor with each other, edifying the industry. Modern marketing and public relations techniques aroused America to the many virtues of wine as an accompaniment to food. As if to emphasize the point, top-rate restaurateurs came to the Valley, offering a variety of gustatory adventures.

Today's Napa Valley, a tourist destination par excellence as well as an ideal place to live, has some 200 wineries, many of them small, ultra-premium gems. Its major cities - Napa, Yountville, St. Helena and Calistoga - still retain much of their 19th Century flavor, tempting the visitor to learn more about their fascinating story.

PHOTO COURTESY OF CAROLINE MARTINI

The Baggy Brigade

Pictured here are many of the winemakers who ushered the Napa Valley through the post-prohibition era and set the foundations for the Valley's current prosperity. Left to right: Brother Tim, Christian Brothers; Charles B. Forni, Sunny St. Helena (Co-op); Walter Sullivan and Aldo Fabrini, Beaulieu Vineyards; Michael Ahearn, Freemark Abbey; Peter & Robert Mondavi, Charles Krug; John Daniel Jr., Inglenook; Louis M. Martini, Martini Winery; Charlie Beringer, Beringer; Martin Stelling, Sunny St. Helena; and Fred Abruzzini, Beringer.

transition: mike grgich

Mike Grgich, currently of Grgich Hills Winery, crafted the winning white wine back then~a 1973 Chateau Montelena Chardonnay. Reflecting on that time, he shares his story.

I was happy and surprised when I heard the news. A friend of mine from Germany called me to tell me I was on television. I didn't know about the tasting because we had not been asked to put the wine into it. I later learned Steven Spurrier smuggled the wines into France. But at that point, it was the biggest excitement of my life.

TIME magazine called to interview me and I thought, "What kind of mistake did I make?" But they said I did everything right. My wine was judged best in Paris. Although I knew my wine was good, not everyone would think so. Wine is like art, and that Chardonnay became a work of art when the critics said so. Then I understood in a moment what it means to be born again and I proved to myself that I could make one of the finest wines in the world.

I had successes before: my 1969 Robert Mondavi Cabernet Sauvignon was proclaimed best in California, but the Paris Tasting was recognition that could go no higher. I'm very shy and the publicity was difficult. In my country, we write "i" in small letters and YOU in large letters. I was educated to minimize myself so I just wanted to continue to do my best after that.

So when my first wine at Grgich Hills, the 1977 Chardonnay, was proclaimed the world's best in Chicago out of 221 Chardonnays from around the world, then it came full circle.

The real feather in my beret is only recent. I went back to Croatia, after communism had forced me to leave 48 years ago, and opened a winery there. But most sweet for me is that I finally got my diploma in enology.

— By Laura Lee Madonna

The Paris

May 24, 1976

The 1976 Paris Tasting stunned the international wine community. As momentum was building in the early 1970's for Napa Valley wine, the Paris Tasting placed the Valley squarely on the map of world class contenders.

Two upstarts toppled elite French wines for first place in that blind tasting arranged by Steven Spurrier, a British wine merchant, resulting in a confirmation of

Tasting

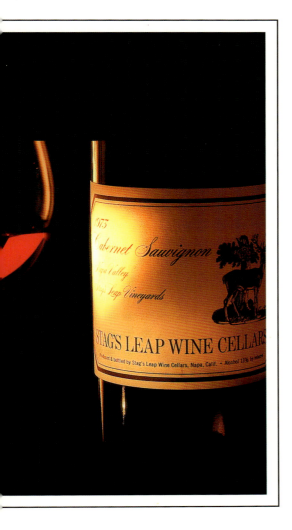

excellence that many already knew.

Those winning sips reverberated around the world though the biggest impact occurred in Napa Valley. Influencing its future wines, it equally impacted its two winning winemakers, Mike Grgich and Warren Winiarski.

A transformation begun, the Valley has never retreated.

epiphany: warren winarski

The 1973 Stag's Leap Wine Cellars Cabernet Sauvignon that Steven Spurrier tasted in our home in the Napa Valley went to Paris dressed as hand luggage for a group of Wine Country tourists. In their true garb as wine bottles, they might not even have crossed the border. So one could say that it is only because of disguised identity that Californian wines came to France at all.

My wife Barbara and I had, in fact, forgotten about handing over the bottles of our 1973 Cabernet to Steven. We were not waiting for the results of any tasting that afternoon when Dorothy Tchelitscheff called to say that our wine had been preferred by the consensus of that distinguished group of tasters over Mouton-Rothschild 1970, Haut-Brion 1970, Lèoville-Las-Cases 1971, Ridge Vineyards 1971 Mountain Range, Heitz Cellar 1970 Martha's Vineyard, and other fine Californian Cabernets. This was a blind tasting – the tasters did not know which wines they were evaluating – another disguised identity.

Like all large and sudden flashes of light, the Paris Tasting was an occurrence with the power to blind. Californians especially were dazzled by the outcome, but the love and the labor lavished on the grapes and the wines of California grew a thousand-fold after the Paris Tasting as the winemakers of California (and elsewhere in the world outside of the "hallowed" soils of France) encouraged and even emboldened by the results, stretched their visions more distantly. In France too, the results sounded a bell to have "another look" and signaled a need to confront a complacency regarding the hierarchy of the world's wines.

Some of this story was examined at the Smithsonian Institution Natural Museum of American History in a symposium entitled "Red, White and American," which commemorated the 20th Anniversary of the Paris Tasting in 1996. This commemorative event was also the occasion of receiving into the institution's permanent collection, a bottle of the Montelena 1973 Chardonnay and the Stag's Leap Wine Cellars 1973 Cabernet Sauvignon.

Into the Future

by
Robert Mondavi

I started my wine growing career in Napa Valley about two generations ago, after my parents moved the family to California in the 1920's. While the valley was as beautiful as it is today, walnuts and prunes were more likely to be found than classic wine grape varieties. When we entered the wine making business, it was a time when wine critics, the wine trade and wine consumers nearly unanimously agreed that the only internationally-accepted fine wines were grown in Europe.

I had been in the wine business 25 years when I challenged that concept. I knew that Napa Valley possesses the climate the soil and the grape varieties to produce wine that ranked with the fine wines of the world. I would pass by Beaulieu Vineyards, with Andre Tschelistcheff; Inglenook, with John Daniel; the Martini Winery and Larkmead, with the Salmina family, and acknowledge that they were improving the situation.

Now, as we reach the end of the millennium, much of the basic research and work has been done, although there is much more to do. We are making fine wines that rank the best in the world, and even more, we are able to make fine wines in the Napa Valley more consistently than any wine region in the world because of the exceptional climate.

For example, research at the University of California at Davis on the soils and climates throughout the world indicates that the center section of the Napa Valley is the best for growing Cabernet Sauvignon. Now we have adopted a natural wine growing philosophy with environmental protection, improved grape quality and worker health as the primary goals.

Where will this lead us in the future? First and most importantly, we are learning to grow our grapes and make our wines naturally which will greatly enhance wine quality. We will grow fruit which more fully expresses our outstanding climate and soil - fruit with greater concentration of flavors, aroma and color with more distinct varietal character. These will be balanced wines with great finesse and complexity that truly complement, not overwhelm the foods they are meant to accompany.

Napa Valley is becoming the world's greatest center for fine wines and fine foods. With 250 wineries, great restaurants and gastronomic institutions, its future has never been brighter as illustrated by Jerry Alexander's fine photo coverage.

SHAFER VINEYARDS,
STAG'S LEAP

Terroir   Dewitt Garlock *Grower Relations, Robert Mondavi Winery*

The word "terroir" has always intrigued and mystified me. Any French vigneron will tell you that the term doesn't have a clear definition. As a scientist, this has always been hard for me to accept. However, it wasn't until I recently found myself gazing into a microscope in the lab of a noted Burgundian soil specialist that it began to make sense to me.

"Look at the worms! They are eating the rock!", Dr. Claude Bourgogne exclaimed with no small amount of enthusiasm. (Remarkably, this irony was not lost on me that a noted Burgundian scientist with the same last name as his homeland would begin to convince me the terroir is truly more that a state of mind!) Indeed, as I looked into the microscope there were worms feeding on the limestone rock. As the professor explained they were turning the rock into fabulous "marle" soil that the French hold in such high regard, producing the great Pinot Noirs and Chardonnays from the Cote d' Or.

So what did Burgundian rock eating worms have to do with the Napa Valley, California, a place seven thousand miles away from this professor's laboratory? The answer suddenly became obvious to me. What is unique to France is just that – unique to France. Those worms probably wouldn't do well in Napa,

I thought as I took another look. Even if I could somehow smuggle a few home with me, there is practically no limestone here for them to feed on and they would surely starve to death! Whatever lives in our soils is unique to the Napa valley just as it is in other great wine districts in California and throughout the world.

The trick to understanding terroir, I surmised, is to learn as much as possible about what the sources of uniqueness are in our own little corner of the world. Then we can coax a more improved wine from the soils by modifying what can and should be modified. And those factors that cannot or should not be changed, we accept. Our soils are different, our climate is different and our land is different. They are most certainly not duplicated anywhere else in the world. The pursuit of understanding these uniqueness is a wonderful blend of science, intuitiveness, mystique and pure enjoyment!

As the Napa Valley continues to mature as one of the great wine growing regions of the world, our discoveries of the different terroir of each sub-appellation, each vineyard site and even specific areas within each vineyard will grow in number. This knowledge will lead to incredibly exciting wines in the years to come.

CHARLES KRUG, ST. HELENA

CARNEROS DISTRICT

Diversity

Robert Steinhauer   *Vineyard Manager, Beringer Vineyards*

Napa Valley is one of the best places on earth for growing grapes because of the excellence and diversity of its climate and soils. That diversity makes my job both challenging and interesting, even after two decades here. We are privileged to farm vineyards in nearly every area within Napa Valley, which allows us to adjust the grape variety we plant to the specific climate and soil of each area.

Napa Valley enjoys a Mediterranean climate, but one highly influenced by the Pacific Ocean. We get rains in winter, when the vines need to be nourished, but we typically have dry weather in summer and through harvest. And we have warm days but cool nights – ideal conditions for growing grapes anywhere, because this temperature fluctuation allows the grapes' sugars to develop but maintains their balancing acids. That balance is what makes for great wine.

Small as Napa Valley is, there is significant climatic variation within it. We believe there are as many as 300 or more distinct climate zones in areas as small as a single vineyard or even a block within a vineyard. The southern end of the valley—from the Carneros appellation up through Napa—is relatively cool and windy because of its proximity to San Pablo Bay. It can be 3 to 5 degrees cooler here than in areas to the north, such as Rutherford and St. Helena. The influences of that climate are very dramatic on the flavor constituents in the grapes. We've learned that this cooler climate is right for Chardonnay and Pinot Noir. This cool climate also produces very fine Merlot.

In contrast, we feel that Cabernet Sauvignon and Sauvignon Blanc need a little more warmth for ripening, so we grow these grapes from the Oakville area north through St. Helena. Another area we think is highly desirable for Cabernet Sauvignon, as well as Merlot and Cabernet Franc, is the Howell Mountain appellation, which starts at an elevation of 1,400 feet, above the summertime fog level, and continues to the mountain's peak.

Napa Valley is made up primarily of soils of volcanic origin: mountain soils that are very rocky and gravelly, and alluvial fans, where the soils were deposited during the glacier age or during periods of very high runoff a million or more years ago. Heavy materials—rock, sand and gravel—were deposited in those periods, and we find these soils very conducive to high-quality fruit because they provide good drainage which helps provide balance between vine and crop growth. When the grapes are ready to mature, we want the vine to be under a certain amount of stress so it stops producing leaves and puts its energy into ripening the fruit. During this period, we don't want the vine to lack water completely, but we don't want it to have too much water.

At one of our prime Cabernet vineyards, Chabot Vineyard, we can actually see exactly where each of the three major soil types in this 32-acre vineyard begin and end as the grapes move toward optimal ripeness. Because the soil type affects the maturation rate, we go back to this vineyard four or five times to pick each area when the fruit there is perfect. Because synergistic relationships like soil and climate, each site, each vineyard, indeed each block within a vineyard, is unique.

FAR LEFT, NEWTON VINEYARDS

UPPER, CARNEROS DISTRICT

LEFT, SPRING BLOOM

BELOW, SPRING VINEYARD, CALISTOGA

LEFT, COVER CROP, FAR NIENTE

STAG'S LEAP

Appellations   John Shafer, *Owner Shafer Vineyards*

In the early '70's when I decided to leave the publishing world in Chicago and pursue a second career in grape growing, I read everything I could find on the subject and came to the conclusion that if I were to do it, I'd want hillside land for the high quality grapes that hillsides produced. So in the spring of 1972 I came to Napa Valley to prospect vineyard sites and found that the few properties available were primarily on the valley floor. But I was determined to find hillside land and eventually stumbled on a property that had been on the market for three years in what is now the Stags Leap District. The 209 acres included a run-down vineyard of Golden Chasselas, Carignane and Zinfandel, last planted in 1922. Before purchasing, I consulted a number of local experts as to its vineyard potential. Laurie Wood of Freemark Abbey tested the soil, looked at the exposure and told me it would be great for Cabernet.

Although Nathan Fay first planted Cabernet in Stags Leap back in 1961, the region's potential for that grape was not recognized until the middle 70's when Clos du Val and Stag's Leap Wine Cellars released their first wines. After owning the vineyard several years, my home winemaking and the increasing interest in our grape growing region, convinced me to replant it to Cabernet Sauvignon and to start a winery. The wine we produced from our hillside vineyards showed the same intense fruit and velvety texture year after year, and it became our signature wine, the Hillside Select Cabernet Sauvignon.

By the early 1980's it was apparent in countless discussions with the media, trade and customers that all of the Cabernets in this Stags Leap region shared similar rich fruit and soft tannins. The name was historic, going back to 1890, and since the wines from the area shared distinct characteristics, I chaired a committee of growers and vintners to petition BATF for the Stags Leap District appellation – approved in 1989.

OPPOSITE, VINEYARD, CALISTOGA

MOUTAINSIDE VINEYARD, CALISTOGA

FALL, NAPA VALLEY

THREE PALMS VINEYARD, CALISTOGA

FALL, NAPA VALLEY

LATE SUMMER,
ST. HELENA

The Independent Winegrape Grower

Andy Beckstoffer   *Owner, Beckstoffer Vineyards*

The independent grape grower may be the least understood hero of the historic increase in winegrape and wine quality in the Napa Valley. State of California statistics indicate that approximately 60% of the grapes harvested in the Napa Valley are grown by vineyardists who do not make the wine – the independent grape growers. The independent grape growers not only produce the majority of the winegrapes, but also farm some of its most prestigious and historic vineyards. Martha's Vineyard, the remaining vineyards first planted by Dr. George Belden Crane, a significant portion of Hamilton Crabb's historic To-Kalon Vineyard, Georges De Latour's original vineyard No.3, Joseph W. Osborne's historic Oak Knoll Ranch are all owned and farmed by growers who do not produce wine. The importance of these growers and their attitudes and activities in the field magnifies with the ever-increasing understanding of the contribution that winegrapes make to the quality of the wine.

The independent grower focuses entirely on the production of top quality fruit and the preservation of the land and its environment. The winery owner of vineyards must share his attention with the winemaking process and the rigors of satisfying the ever-changing consumer market. This clear focus makes the independent grower the major long-term defender and developer of grape quality and cleanliness of his environment.

The concept of what has been called "sustainable agriculture" outlines well the goals of the independent grower. Sustainable agriculture integrates the goals of environmental health, economic profitability and social and economic equity.

In achieving these goals, the non-winery grower is held to a special standard with regard to grape quality. The independent grower must sell all of his production. He does not have an anonymous wine blend in which he can "lose" a bad lot of grapes. High quality grape production is his only long-term solution to economic viability in an unstable market. Since the independent grower sells only grapes, he cannot lose money on the grape sale and make it up on the sale of the wine.

Again, his only long-term solution is the highest possible grape quality.

The first wave of grape growing families who came to the Napa Valley in the mid-19th Century understood that in the Napa Valley with its fertile alluvial soils and Mediterranean climate, the solution to the problems meant greater quality not more quantity. George Belden Crane, Hamilton Crabb, Joseph Osborne and the others dismissed the high tonnage Mission grape and began planting varietals. Andre Tchelistcheff, the Mondavis, John Daniel and others of the second wave in the 1930's brought the same attitude with their advanced vineyard and winery practices. The third wave of vineyardists in the 1960's and early 1970's again sought better quality grapes through globally researched advanced vineyard practices and technologies. In each wave, the independent grower has played a major part in making the Napa Valley and its grapes and wines what they are today and what they will be tomorrow.

MT. ST. HELENA, CALISTOGA

Pruning begins after the first real frost until the first days of March. Pruning serves two main purposes: crop yield and to establish or maintain the shape of the plant – this making normal vineyard practices easier. Typically we do two types of pruning based on the type of trellis system: "spur pruning" (seen here) leaves the two buds per shoot that will produce two new canes, normally yielding two clusters of grapes per cane. "Cane pruning" leaves longer canes, normally one per side of the vine – six to eight buds per cane. Each of these buds will in turn produce a new cane, generally yielding two clusters each (as with spur pruning).

PHOTO BY LAURA HUNT

Taste

Pairing

Sarah Scott
Executive Chef, Robert Mondavi Winery

When I moved to the Napa Valley in 1979, my idea of a great meal was a bottle of Blue Nun and a thick, juicy steak. Together. Living here has changed my life dramatically.

I arrived fresh from college in Atlanta with a journalism degree in hand. A rejection from the local newspaper turned me toward the food business, my other interest. After working in a couple of local restaurants, now long gone, I realized I had found my calling. Cooking grabbed hold of me and hasn't let me loose since.

With the support and encouragement of many local foodies and wonderful friends, I started a catering business in the mid-80's. As it turns out, this was about the same time that many wineries were getting into exploring wine and food pairing as a great way to showcase their wines. As a caterer working with these wineries, I got the op-

FARMER'S MARKET, ST. HELENA

portunity to participate in many tastings where we would sit before an array of wines and foods with the goal of finding the perfect marriage. These sessions were enlightening, educational and ultimately, inebriating. And while perfect marriages are hard to come by, many pairings were successful and while we realized it is not so cut and dry, generally wonderfully balanced wines tend to go with well-balanced dishes. It seems that red wines, usually heavier bodied wines, tend to enhance heartier foods and flavors, and that white wines, usually lighter in body, compliment lighter flavors and ingredients. Most importantly, the less stress about it all makes for the best meal.

After 20 years of living in the Napa Valley, it feels like home. These vineyards and their cycles have become a part of me and guide my sensibilities in cooking and living. And now, as a chef for Robert Mondavi Winery, I get the wonderful opportunity to share this very special place with people all over the world - the wines, the food and the life we live in this valley.

I still love those steak dinners, but have come to prefer them with a great bottle of Cabernet Sauvignon. Sorry Sister.

SARAH SCOTT

Pioneers

Gary Jenanyan
Executive Chef, Culinary Consultant

The extraordinary fresh flavors on Napa Valley tables did not just happen overnight. The genesis for our international reputation for taste occurred more than 20 years ago, beginning on the tables of a handful of culinary pioneers, mostly women.

These women, many of them matriarchs of wine making and wine growing families, planted the first seeds of taste, both literally and figuratively. The most notable are Belle Rhodes, the Trefethens, Margrit Biever Mondavi, Virginia Van Asperen, Martha May, Barbara Eisele, Molly Chappellet, and Dolores Cakebread.

Their early insistence on better, fresher ingredients mirrored the winemakers' quest for more refined, more drinkable, less intellectual wines.

We also have pioneering Napa Valley chefs such as Udo Nechutnys, Phillipe Jeanty, Emily Didier, Annie Roberts, Bruce LeFavor and Jamie Morningstar Bertoli as well as growers Forni-Brown and organic produce advocate Sibella Kraus to thank for starting the movement towards higher quality ingredients. Those of us now cooking and entertaining here, the old and new guards, are all benefactors of their early vision. So are the guests at our tables.

BILL BRIWA, CULINARY INSTITUTE OF AMERICA AT GREYSTONE

In the mid-1970's I worked under pioneering chefs, Michael James and Catherine Brandel and helped procure the ingredients for the 3-star French chefs visiting the Robert Mondavi Winery. Ingredients such as fresh rabbit, lamb, duck, squab, pig, free-range chicken, goat cheese, herbs, lettuce and olive oil were simply not available locally then. Now all of those items are grown or produced within an hour's drive.

Happily, today the taste of Napa Valley encompasses our wines, our restaurants and winery tables, our cooking schools and our world-class produce. We have much for which to be thankful and proud.

MARCO IN THE GARDEN

FOLLOWING PAGES, OAKVILLE GROCERY

WAPPO BAR & BISTRO

Startup

Michelle Mutrux & Arron Bauman
Chefs/Owners, Wappo Bar & Bistro

In the early days of dreaming of the restaurant that someday we might have, we thought of the food we would serve as something quite different from the usual wine country cuisine. The sort of northern Italian/California/Pacific Rim fare served in minuscule portions, where one ate with the eyes but left with a curious hunger in the soul. Truly, living in Northern California with virtually every foodstuff in the world at your fingertips, we asked ourselves, why limit oneself to a particular cuisine? Why couldn't we serve a Persian Fesanjan on the same menu as Paella Valenciana? If the menu was based on seasonal availability

continues on next page

Emily

Amy Wend   *Owner, Skyhill Farms*

Living and grazing on 48 acres nestled high in the Carneros Hills above the Napa Valley we find doe-eyed Emily and her pals, Rose and Natalie. These three were the foundation of the Skyhill herd of over 500 goats today. While the three ladies were preparing for their new career of supplying milk to the Skyhill plant, Ted and I were busy planting organic gardens. The fresh fruits and vegetables harvested for the terraced hillsides were sold to the farmers' markets and plans were formalized to build a state-of-the-art cheese plant and milking parlor.

By 1989 Emily's group had increased to 50 and the first cheese logs were produced. Today she sells her cheeses and yogurts nationwide with her picture proudly featured on all the products. She still loves the camera. Emily insists that we practice the artisan style of cheese making. Each day's fresh goat's milk is carefully transferred from the chilled stainless steel holding tank into a 300 gallon cheese making vat. The milk is pasteurized, vegetable cultures are added and the cheese making process begins. The finished cheese curd is hung in cheese cloth bags draining excess whey. The cheese is then artistically flavored, salted and formed into individual cheese logs. Emily is now ready for her product and her picture to go to the market.

and the plates themselves were culturally grounded and produced as authentically as possible within their vernacular context – could it work? There were no laws written or non-written that we knew of. Thinking in a broad "end of the Millennium" terms it could be considered "timely", with the increasing globalization and interconnectedness that the world is coming to understand. In any case we were two undercapitalized chefs itching to express ourselves in a small venue in a small town at the top of the Napa Valley.

Ninety percent of restaurants fail within the first year, or so we were often told. In retrospect we certainly threw all caution to the wind and went for it with open hearts and sincere enthusiasm. Not blindly, we were forewarned and willing to give what it takes to run a restaurant six days a week. Maybe we were a little foolish to think we could be a success in a place where some of our betters had failed. Fortunately, we had luck, the support of the whole community—and what a better place in the world to be chefs, than the Napa Valley?

Perhaps the most often asked question (besides "what do you put in the water") is what does "wappo" mean? When we decided to focus on the indigenous cuisines of the world, we asked ourselves what was indigenous to the Napa Valley? Certainly not wine and grapes. So we thought of the people who once inhabited this beautiful place, and thought it appropriate to dedicate to Napa's first people.

We subsequently found that there are many descendents of the "Wappo" Mishewal Clan. That they are living quietly throughout Sonoma, Alexander Valley, and Lake County areas. Originally, they were given the brand name "Guapo" by the Spanish, meaning handsome, brave, or in their particular case, invincible. Through the sequence of time and many diverse dinners we learned that in Uruguay wappo means someone who is very hard working. In Neopolitano dialect, wappo means a tough guy who has a heart. But in the end we simply liked how the words Wappo Bar Bistro sounded together... and so it is.

The Independent Winemaker

Karen Culler

When I came to the Napa Valley in 1984, it was an exciting time for the wine industry. At that time, wineries were fairly prosperous. Everyone was investing in expansion, and more importantly, in winery improvements to enhance wine quality. We spent much of our time and resources researching Old World traditions of wine making, and figuring out the best way to combine these with the new efficient equipment and technology. Once we felt confident with our improvements in the winery, we moved on to changes in the vineyard. These viticultural changes firmly

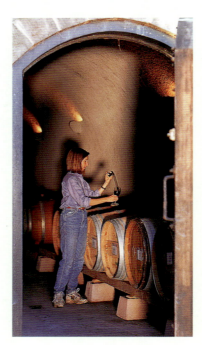

KAREN CULLER

rooted Napa Valley's place with the top of the wine growing regions of the world.

During this time, the structures of wineries were also evolving. Many wineries were growing and others were consolidating. It seemed as if the climate in Napa valley was changing to one of larger wineries, and the agricultural flavor was disappearing. Although this was what everyone reads about in the wine magazines, there is an increasing growth in the number of small wine producers within the Napa Valley. These are vendors who are drawn to unique vineyards, producing high quality grapes and ultimately premium wines. Some are grape growers who recognize that their vineyard is a cut above the others. Some are winemakers who want to make a statement with their own wines. These winemakers are highlighting the characteristics of particular vineyards, region and terroirs, which makes the wines special. They are people making wines without the benefit of tastings rooms or a public relations representative.

These hidden winemakers, making small quantities of wine in nondescript buildings tucked in amongst the glamorous wineries, share a healthy camaraderie with the better known vintners and all contribute to the diversity that will maintain Napa Valley's position as a world-class producer of wine.

We have so far identified more than 80, out of a probable 1000, components in wine . The object of wine tasting is to assess a wine's quality.

Professional tastings involve making notes to discern the wine's color, aroma (or bouquet for more mature wines) and once in the mouth considerations to note are fizziness , viscosity, tannins, acidity and sweetness. Wines between 59° and 68° are ideal for tasting. Generally a blind tasting (not knowing brand names) is the only way to achieve an unbiased report.

Most of us "taste" for pleasure and that needs only a willingness to suspend prejudgements and an open mind.

Wine bottles come in an array of sizes, often with exotic and tongue twisting names. The vessels shown above possess the classic bordeaux shape. Sizes larger than a magnum are usually produced in limited quantities.

(opposite)
Distilling wine to make top quality brandy requires many important decisions. Essentially the distiller is trying to separate the constituents of the wine by partial vaporization and then separately recovering the vapor and the residue. But herein lies the art for there is a crucial balance between how efficient the process and how interesting the final product will be. It seems the fewer impurities the less interesting.

The number of times the juice is distilled (usually two or more times) also contributes to the ultimate quality. Distillation speed is also important. Pot distillation (shown here at the RMS Alambic Distillery in Caneros) enable the distiller to have more precise control of the entire process. The next step—maturing the distillate in oak barrels—plays a crucial role in the final flavors.

Tools

The "clone wood" is selected from healthy vines in the late summer. Each "bud" is then chosen by size to exactly fit the rootstock.

Above, below, opposite: We will graft the rootstock immediatly after gathering the budwood, whenever possible. Selecting the right size "bud" using the grafter's tools to precisely fit the rootstock's incision is called field budding.

Clones

John Cauldwell
Winegrower & President, Cauldwell Nursery

We need to make sure that our vineyards are world class. Our wines are put up against the best that the French and the Italians have to offer. Australia and Chile are getting better all the time. One way we can continue to improve is by making good, sound decisions in choosing the very best material available to put into the vineyard. Proper clonal selection is an important key.

Within a single grape variety, there is a rich variation of subtle differences manifested by their growth habit and grape berry character. Examples of this include the tricolored berries of the Pinot family (Pinot Noir, Pinot Blanc and Pinot Gris) and the occasional muscat-flavored berries found in some Chardonnay vines.

From the earliest beginning of grape growing, people have been selecting the wood from their best vines when planting new ones. In modern times, concerns about grapevine health and fruit quality have led to a process called clonal selection. In viticulture, a clone is a population of vines derived by vegetative propagation from a single vine. We call this the mother vine. All the vines grown from cuttings of buds of the mother vine are identical. And all future generations will remain identical unless a spontaneous mutation occurs.

Clonal selection began in Germany in 1926 and now takes place in most grape growing countries in order to supply growers with the best possible planting material. In France 80% of new vineyards are planted with clonal selections of both root stock and scions.

The right clonal selections can only complement the important influence of "terroir" which is the basis of wine style diversity within every region.

Bench grafting takes place indoors and has become more popular recently. It also allows for precise matching of the scion and the root stock cutting by using a grafting machine. Once the fitting is complete the root stocks are placed in boxes of moist, coarse "soil" and stored for two weeks in rooms at 82 degrees. Once the bud has callused the grafts are waxed (opposite, lower left) to cut down moisture loss. Next stop is to plant them, usually in a nursery. Once a good root system has developed they are now ready for their new vineyard home.

Growing tubes are a recent addition to our vineyards. Coming from New Zealand and Australia they serve some useful purposes. They protect the young vine from rabbits and other rodents, protect against the wind and offer a greenhouse effect increasing the growth of the wine in the first year.

Training the young vine (below right) is one of the most important activities for the grower. It helps determine the trellis system and ultimately crop yields and vineyard operation practices.

H
A
R
V
E
S
T

MEASURING BRIX WITH A REFRACTOMETER

The Tools of the Trade

Gail Chablis   *Wine Writer, Napa Valley*

It's early morning on a crisp September morning. The sky is clear and there is no sign of any lingering morning dew. Geoff Murray, wine maker, and Chris Corley, assistant wine maker at Monticello Vineyards, prepare to walk the vineyards and collect grape samples to test the sugar levels.

The brix scaling system is predominant throughout the Napa Valley and the U.S. and many within the industry unconsciously interchange the word brix to refer to sugar levels. When I first met Geoff, his dedication to quality was very apparent. Analytical in nature, he graciously shared his personal preferences and methods for sampling and testing the sugar using the refractometer and hydrometer – two simple but essential tools.

Wine makers use the refractometer (a small telescope-looking gadget) out in the vineyard or lab to gauge the sugar level using refractive measurements (the measurement of density using light influenced by temperature). The hydrometer is a glass tube that is weighted at the end that measures juice density. The hydrometer is placed inside a breaker filled with grape juice. The density of the juice, when adjusted for temperature, determines the amount of sugar.

In any one sampling, Geoff will hand select up to 250 berries from different clusters from throughout Monticello's 80 acres of estate grown chardonnay, merlot, pinot noir and cabernet.

Although the refractometer can be used on-site at the vineyard, Geoff says most wine makers collect their berry of cluster samples and conduct all the testing back at the lab using both the refractometer and the hydrometer.

"What is the final test?"

"The final test is the flavor," Geoff says. "Does the fruit taste ripe. Does it taste green. Is it ready to pick?" The end result is evidenced by tasting, which always reveals the truth.

PREVIOUS PAGE, STAGLIN FAMILY VINEYARDS

STAGLIN FAMILY VINEYARDS

STAG'S 'S LEAP "SLV" VINEYARD

FOLLOWING PAGE, FAY VINEYARD,
STAG'S LEAP WINE CELLARS

RUTHERFORD HILL VINEYARD

HAIKU

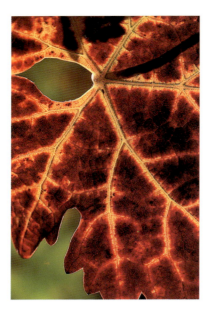

Colors of Nature
the hand of the Creator
earth divine, red wine.

– Izu Baiko

PHOTO BY AVA MIRANDA

The grapes are taken from the field to the hopper as soon as they are picked. The harvest generally begins at first light.

A few wineries will hand examine the grapes before being crushed such as at Stag's Leap Wine Cellars (left).

From here the juice goes into a freshly prepared fermentation tank (opposite top/center), and the stems go into a container to be put back into the field or disposed of. Some wines, usually Chardonnay, may be fermented in oak barrels.

There are many ways to filter wine—from using egg whites, (normally called fining) to sophisticated machines. Wineries filter to strain solid particles out of the wine (opposite lower right). Red wines long aged in barrels can often avoid filtration. Some wineries will believe this can rob the wine of complexity. An unfiltered wine will generally say so on the label.

MARCO CAPPELI,
SWANSON WINERY

RUTHERFORD
HILL WINERY

ROBERTO,
SWANSON WINERY

SWANSON WINERY

BARRELS

Marco Capelli   Wine Maker, Swanson Vineyards

The use of oak barrels in wine production has evolved to its current frenzy from very humble beginnings. Once used mainly for storage and transport, oak barrels now play a critical role in enhancing the aromatic and flavor complexity of wines of every conceivable origin and price level.

In 1990, we began an oak-seasoning program unique to our vines and aimed ultimately at creating wines with an oak character. Since then, we have been sourcing wood from forests in the Northeastern U.S. and seasoning the green, rough-cut staves outside in the elements for a minimum of three years. This time period in the open air helps eliminate the sappy, resinous components in the wood, while leaving behind much of the desirable, sweet vanilla flavors. After seasoning, the staves are taken to a local cooper where they are bent into shape and toasted over a wood fire according to our specific instructions.

While we ask ourselves often if it wouldn't be easier to just buy commercially available barrels (at a lower price) for all our production. The results of our project have been too encouraging to ignore: delicious oak flavors and aromas unique to our wines, and the comfort of total control.

Opposite,
The staves for the
barrels being
seasoned.

Right,
The metal hoops being
fitted onto a barrel,
while in the foreground
a barrel is being heated
in preparation for being
shaped.

Left,
Wood chips burning in a
vented metal firepot called
a "chaufferette." The barrels are placed over the
chaufferette to heat so the
staves may be bent. There
are many ways to provide
this heat, such as steam or
boiling water, but many
winemakers prefer using
barrels made using the
chaufferette because of the
toasting that occurs. The
amount of toasting can be
varied, resulting in different flavorings when the
wine is being aged in the
barrels.

STAG'S LEAP WINE CELLARS

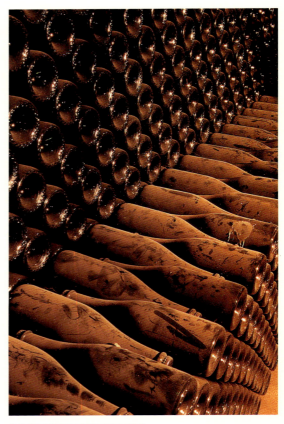

SCHRAMSBERG VINEYARDS

DEAN & DELUCA MARKET

Another View...

Father John Brenkle
St. Helena Catholic Church

It's hard to sleep comfortably when you can see from your bedroom window a half dozen men bedding down outside on a porch floor.

A couple years ago this number of "campers" at St. Helena Catholic Church was as high as twenty-five. It was then that a few of us determined that we needed to do something. These were not homeless people. These were hard working migrant labors who came to do terribly hard field work that very few of us locals were willing or able to do.

The "romance" of wine growing is attracting millions of tourists to the Napa Valley. But there is nothing romantic about harvesting grapes. It is backbreaking, hot, sticky work. The least we can do is make sure that these workers have a place to clean up, eat and sleep. So a group of us started the *Farm Worker Committee* which has been meeting monthly for the past 8 years.

Our efforts gave rise to a tent camp located at the Carmelite Monastery in Oakville. We

hoped to accommodate some 80 workers, but the objections of the neighbors forced us to limit it to 40. This was to be a one year only solution and it did give us time to negotiate with the Heublein Corporation to acquire the former Christian Bothers camp. The facility was purchased for $1.00 and has become the satellite for our present operations.

Renamed the *Calistoga Farm Center*, we are able to accommodate some 40 workers for 9 months. Likewise, through the graciousness of the Robert Mondavi Winery, we are permitted to manage their facility for up to 30 laborers. We also have five mobile units each accommodating 4 workers.

In 1984 there were 25 privately owned camps operated by our growers and vintners. The number had dwindled down to 9 with a 50% drop in living units. In June of this year Campo Amarillio was razed, reducing by 35 the number of beds.

So once again we are seeing our laborers crowding in with their friends, sleeping in cars or finding a kindly porch. The work of our Farm Workers Committee is more essential than ever. We are committed to do whatever is possible to make sure that those workers are treated with respect and gratitude and to keep our wine industry healthy.

Continued

Arnulfo Solorio, C-89
Vineyard Worker & Supervisor

Twenty years of daily work in the vineyards have granted me a unique relationship with vines. Throughout their seasonal changes I have learned their language. I can anticipate when they are sick, stressed with foliage, or hungry by simply looking at them. During my daily walks through the fields I talk to them, I caress them and I know they listen to me because they produce abundantly.

Vines and I coexist in a symbiotic relationship. My livelihood depends on their product, and they depend on my human care to produce quality grapes.

It is also important to mention the immense gratification and sense of identification one gets from being a wine grower. Working all year long and producing nearly six thousand tons of grapes at the end of harvest is gratifying. Seeing the product of long hours of the work of 80 to 100 men, gives renewed energy to the next season.

Equally important is the identification I draw from the work I do. I recall during an interview earlier this year, I was asked to give feedback about my work, and my response was "C-89 was my identification." (C-89 stands for an area in Carneros district, section 89.) This meant that the area I was in charge of represented the kind of worker I am.

Frost protection is of critical concern in the early spring after bud break. Lighting smudge pots (above) adds as much of 5° warmth to the ambient temperature in a vineyard. This extra amount of heat is usually enough to prevent the young vines from freezing.

Traditions

TASTING ROOM,
LA FAMIGLIA
WINERY

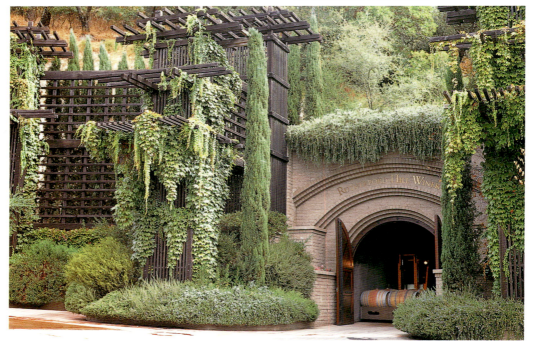

RUTHERFORD HILL WINERY

HESS
COLLECTION
WINERY,
ART ROOM

CLOS DU VAL
WINERY

DREAMING IN NAPA VALLEY

H. William Harlan

The verdant fairways at Meadowood Napa Valley were charged with expectation. Great clusters of green and purple balloon grapes dancing in the warm breezes under the large white tent greeted the bidders arriving at the inaugural Napa Valley Wine Auction in June, 1981.

This was the premier of a dream that meant many things to many people. There was the original vision of Robert and Margrit Mondavi and Pat Montandon to stage a wine auction of international renown. There were the vintners, with the

opportunity to establish an event which would simultaneously promote the wines of Napa Valley, the good health of the valley and communication between vintners, growers, and the community-at-large. There were the remarkable individuals who spent two years planning the first auction. And there, perhaps diminutively by comparison, was my personal dream of Meadowood becoming a common meeting ground for the vintners and growers of the valley.

Since I graduated from college, I had

PHOTO BY BRUCE FLEMING

been searching Napa Valley for a vineyard site from which to produce a fine California "first growth." In the summer of 1979, a friend introduced me to a completely different property – Meadowood, a small country club nestled in an incredibly beautiful little valley just outside St. Helena. It wasn't a vineyard, but it was a jewel. My partners and I consummated the purchase in less than a week.

From the outset our partnership mission was clear. We wanted to make Meadowood the finest country resort in America and a center for the activities of the vintners and growers of this magnificent region.

In the fall of 1979, the Napa Valley Vintners and the Auction Steering Committee began planning the first event. I joined the Steering Committee as did several of our key staff. The selection of a site was paramount. Imagine my excitement when the Committee inquired if we would host the event. I simply said, "Yes, we would be honored."

The rest is a dazzling history. Meadowood has been the home for the Napa Valley Wine Auction ever since. The longevity of this relationship is a source of immense pleasure to me. At Meadowood, we continue to delight in and support the Napa Valley wine growing community and their remarkable contributions to the good life. And by the way, I eventually did find my vineyard.

Full circle.

Whether your mood is for bubbles on a quiet terrace with a wonderful view of the valley, or delighting in a wonderful live jazz performance with a crowd, the Napa Valley offers a full palette of experiences.

The performing arts have been developing a momentum of their own, continually evolving, extending the Valley's oeuvre beyond its world famous reputation for wines & cuisine.

MUMM, NAPA VALLEY

CONCERT, ROBERT MONDAVI WINERY

Living Art

Jamie Davies *Owner, Schramsberg Vineyards*

From the porch, Schrmsberg Vineyards

I was 30 years old when I arrived at the wild expanse of tangled, overgrown vines, poison oak and woodland pressed against the Napa Valley's Mayacamas Mountains. I held a degree in political science from the University of California at Berkeley, had two young sons, aged two and four, and was nine months pregnant with my third.

Only the charm, wit and intelligence of my late husband, Jack, pulled me away from the emerging San Francisco art scene in which I played a seminal role a few years earlier. Once settled in Los Angeles where I was nurturing a young family and Jack's profession, we began planning an escape to the country, to fertile ground for creating something entirely of our own making. The dream has become Schramsberg, the first California winery to make quality sparkling wine following the traditional practices of the Champenoise half a globe away.

I probably never asked myself if there was a limit to my endurance during this 30-year adventure. The natural beauty of Schramsberg spoke to me in a way that nothing else could or would. I assumed a role of stewardship for a place that would bridge economic trials, naysayers and time. Somehow, this fortified me to take on the resurrection of the rundown, rodent-infested Victorian home, untamed gardens, derelict winery and a local wine community that thought the plan of making methode champenoise wines from Napa Valley Chardonnay and Pinot Noir grapes outlandish.

I faced bats in the nursery, snakebites, rabid skunks, countless devilish pranks among the three growing boys, disappearing mother's helpers, an absence of vineyard help and a dearth of fruit required to make our dream American sparkling wine.

Remarkably, our vision of what Schramsberg was and could be has not flagged in three decades. The woodland scene as one ascends the mountain road to Schramsberg is very much as it was in the late 1800s when Robert Louis Stevenson arrived on horseback to visit Jacob Schram. The caves in which Schramsberg sparkling wines are aged and riddled have been improved and expanded, yet have the look and magnificent mold of the ages. The gardens and family home are beautifully maintained, but in no way call attention to themselves.

The young woman who once envisioned and then breathed life into San Francisco's first art fairs, and went on to found her own gallery, has made the place called Schramsberg her greatest living art.

V. SATTUI WINERY

BERINGER VINEYARDS

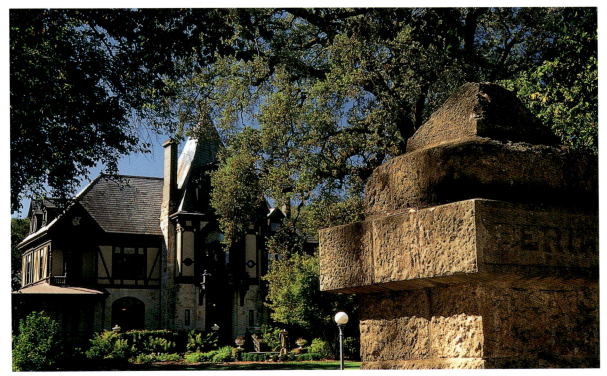

CHATEAU
MONTELENA

NEWTON
VINEYARD

ST. CLEMENT
VINEYARDS

CLOS
PEGASE
WINERY

Leaving the winery crowds behind reveals yet another side to the Valley.

JESSEL GALLERY

OLIVE GROVE, AUBERGE DU SOLEIL

OLIVE GROVE, AUBERGE DU SOLEIL

Art

The arts have found a home in the Napa Valley. Some years ago the idea of world class exhibitions and ongoing art shows was put into place by Rene di Rosa, Margrit Biever Mondavi, and others. Soon we saw the establishment of the Napa Art Council and in 1987 Jessel Miller created the Gallery Association of Napa Valley. Galleries such as Jessel's now represent more than three hundred artists. Permanent displays of the highest mark are now housed at the Hess Winery, Clos Pegase Winery and in the Olive Grove at Auberge du Soleil. Mumm Napa Valley displays ongoing photo shows of the best photographers in the country. The town of Napa will soon have *The Center for Food Wine and the Arts*. Once a year, many Napa Valley artists open their studios giving the visitor an intimate look at art in the Valley. This evolution continues to enhance the Valley's environment.

Many individual vineyards have become noted for their for unique flavors. The To-Kalon vineyard (at the Robert Mondavi Winery) was established in 1868 by Henry Crabb. The word is Greek and means "highest beauty".

Since the earliest days adventurers, writers, poets, artists, (and more than a few scallywags) have been drawn to the intrinsic beauty of the Napa Valley. One of the most wonderful experiences of all is being with friends and watching as the shadows move across the land.

ROBERT MONDAVI WINERY

AUBERGE DU SOLEIL

CROQUET, MEADOWOOD

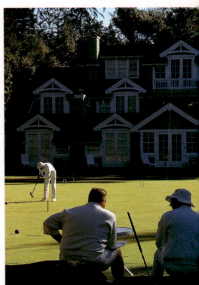

Yountville, Sunrise from a Balloon

PAGES 8-9, 30 MINUTES LATER

In 1954 I was five years old. My mom and dad had decided they wanted to raise my two brothers and me (and later my sister) in the country. We didn't have alot of money back then but they found a piece of property on Silverado Trail in Napa Valley. The parcel was 32 acres but that was beyond our reach. The owner, George Jepsen, could sense how much Mom and Dad wanted to be there so he let them buy just eight acres. We grew up with cows, a couple of horses and even grew prunes in the early days. My brothers and I had to pick the harvest each year. We always tried to find a way out, but Dad couldn't do it alone.

There were less than 25 wineries in the Valley then, and St. Helena and Calistoga seemed a world away. I attended Soda Canyon elementary school, which had only two classrooms: for the first six years I had the same teacher, Mrs. Rae Jones. Never will I forget her!

In 1980 we started a culinary herb and vegetable garden on the property and worked with many of the now famous chefs. Udo Nechutnys, Bruce Lefavor, Catherine Brandel, and Phillipe Jeanty, among many others, would come to the garden to collect (and at times pick) their produce.

In 1982 we planted our first vines and by 1985 our first grape crop went to Vichon Winery. We tried our hand at making wine too. Warren Winiarski at Stag's Leap Wine Cellars traded us the necessary ingredients and his highly tuned wine-making knowledge for my dad's unbelievably sweet white corn. Over the years we have had the pleasure of working with the Robert Mondavi Winery, Duckhorn Vineyards and Swanson Winery.

Working with my family and on the land I grew up on brings immeasurable joy to me. So in thanking everyone who helped with this book, I wish to acknowledge my family first. Loma, my wife, encouraged this project and helped bring light to it, as she does to so many things. Jim Scott, for his vision and creative juice. Chuck O'Rear continues to be my mentor and more importantly my pal. I thank Chris Burt, my publisher and close friend, for his positive attitude. Ave Miranda, a young aspiring photographer from Oregon, came here for two weeks to help me in the field. We spent long days making images (and lots of fun, too). This book is the better because of her help. Sheri Scott, for finding just the right phrase. Thank you, Laura Hunt, for your discerning eye. Thank you, Belle Rhodes for your encouragement. Alexis Swanson's enthusiasm was inspiring. Jesse Miller and I had long talks that helped move this project along; and Carolyn Gamble & JG Heithcock, for the finishing touches! And finally, Izu Baiko, whose poetry has inspired me throughout the years.

Gratefully,